Create and Share | Thinking Digitally

Sharing Photos Online

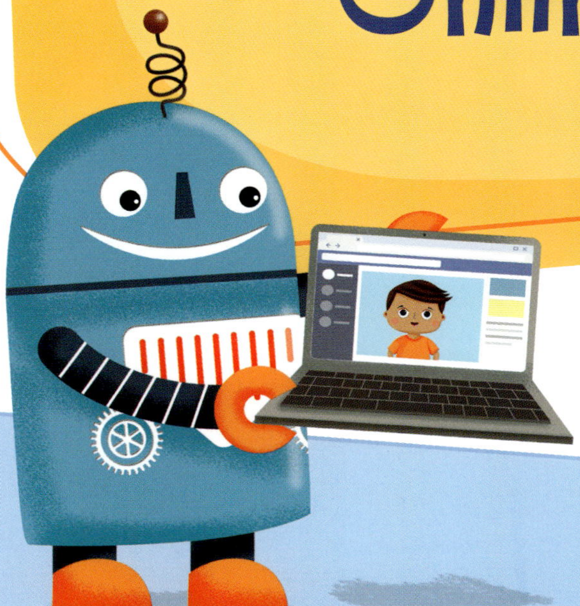

By Amber Lovett

Published in the United States of America by:
Cherry Lake Press
2395 South Huron Parkway, Suite 200, Ann Arbor, Michigan
www.cherrylakepublishing.com

Series Adviser: Kristin Fontichiaro
Reading Adviser: Marla Conn, MS, Ed., Literacy specialist, Read-Ability, Inc.
Book Designer: Felicia Macheske
Character Illustrator: Rachael McLean

Photo Credits: © LightField Studios/Shutterstock.com, 13; © Gorodenkoff/Shutterstock.com, 17; © wavebreakmedia/Shutterstock.com, 19

Graphics Throughout: © the simple surface/Shutterstock.com; © Diana Rich/Shutterstock.com; © lemony/Shutterstock.com; © CojoMoxon/Shutterstock.com; © IreneArt/Shutterstock.com; © Artefficient/Shutterstock.com; © Marie Nimrichterova/Shutterstock.com; © Svetolk/Shutterstock.com; © EV-DA/Shutterstock.com; © briddy/Shutterstock.com; © Mix3r/Shutterstock.com

Library of Congress Cataloging-in-Publication Data

Names: Lovett, Amber, author. | McLean, Rachael, illustrator.
Title: Sharing photos online / by Amber Lovett ; illustrated by Rachael McLean.
Description: Ann Arbor, Michigan : Cherry Lake Publishing, 2020. | Series: Create and share : thinking digitally | Includes index. | Audience: Grades 2-3.
Identifiers: LCCN 2019033412 (print) | LCCN 2019033413 (ebook) | ISBN 9781534159112 (hardcover) | ISBN 9781534161412 (paperback) | ISBN 9781534160262 (pdf) | ISBN 9781534162563 (ebook)
Subjects: LCSH: Photography—Digital techniques—Juvenile literature. | Computer file sharing—Juvenile literature.
Classification: LCC TR267 .L686 2020 (print) | LCC TR267 (ebook) | DDC 777—dc23
LC record available at https://lccn.loc.gov/2019033412
LC ebook record available at https://lccn.loc.gov/2019033413
Cherry Lake Publishing would like to acknowledge the work of the Partnership for 21st Century Learning, a Network of Battelle for Kids. Please visit *www.battelleforkids.org/networks/p21* for more information.

Printed in the United States of America
Corporate Graphics

Cherry Lake Press

Table of

CONTENTS

CHAPTER ONE

Know Your Camera

Say cheese! Grab your camera and get ready to take some pictures. But first, let's talk about cameras. What kinds are there, and how do they work?

What kind of camera do you have at home? You might have a digital camera. These cameras have a display screen that allows you to see the pictures you take. Instant cameras take pictures and print them instantly. Smartphones can take really good pictures too!

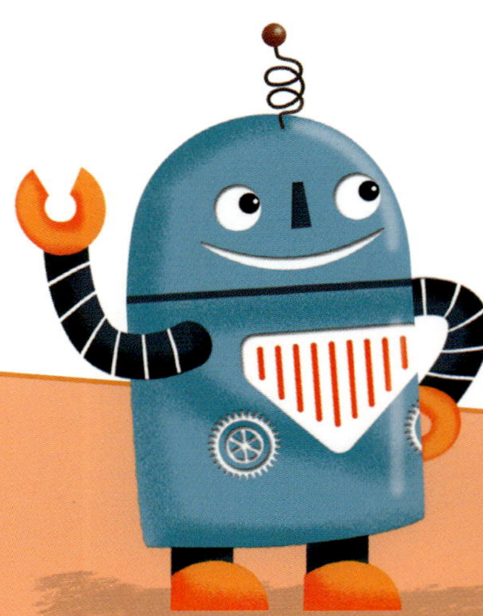

These cameras are all different, but they have a lot in common. Cameras work by capturing light with a **sensor**. The **lens** is like the camera's eye. It **focuses**, or adjusts, the light to make the picture clear. Other parts of the camera help you **filter** how much light is captured. Too much or too little light makes it hard to see the objects in your picture.

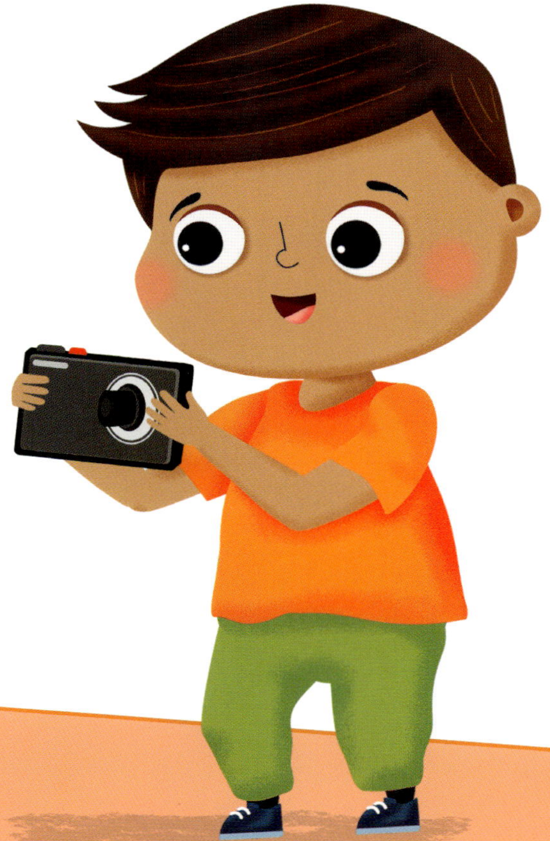

Digital cameras are one of the most common kinds of cameras.

POWER BUTTON: This turns your camera on and off.

SHUTTER: You press this to take a picture.

LENS: This is the eye of the camera. Smartphones have more than one lens. One is in the back of the phone, and one is in the front, for selfies.

ZOOM: Your camera might have a zoom button. This makes the objects you're shooting appear closer or farther away. On a smartphone, pinch the screen with your fingers to zoom in or out.

FLASH: This acts like a flashlight. Turn the flash on when your pictures are too dark.

DISPLAY PANEL: This screen shows you what your camera sees.

PORT: A place in a camera or phone that allows you to connect it to a computer or charger.

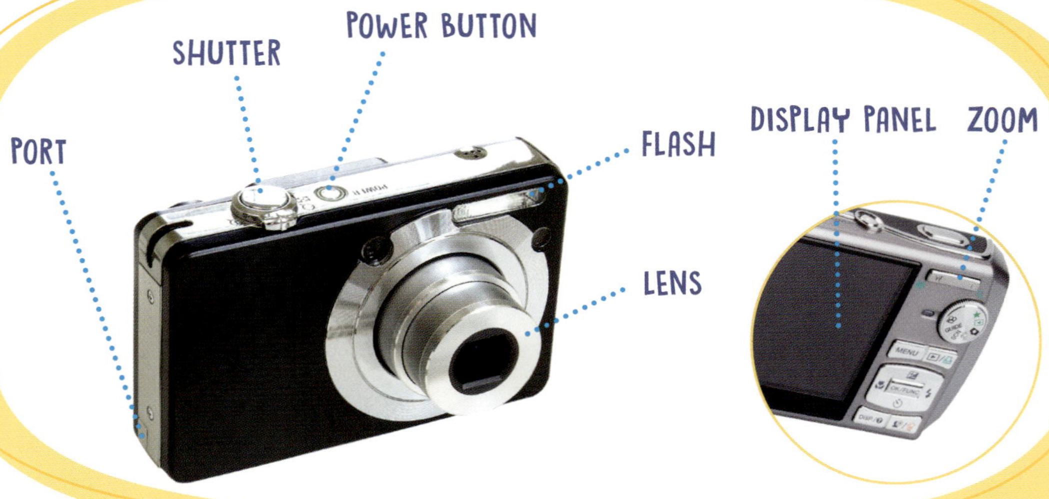

ACTIVITY

Get to Know Your Camera

Look at your camera. What kind is it? Is it a smartphone? Is it a digital or instant camera? Next, look at the buttons on the camera. Try each button out to see what it does. Answer these questions to make sure you know your camera:

- What button do you press to take a photo?
- How do you see what the photo you took looks like?
- How do you zoom in and out?
- How do you turn on the flash in your camera?
- If you are using a smartphone, how do you switch from selfie mode to regular mode?

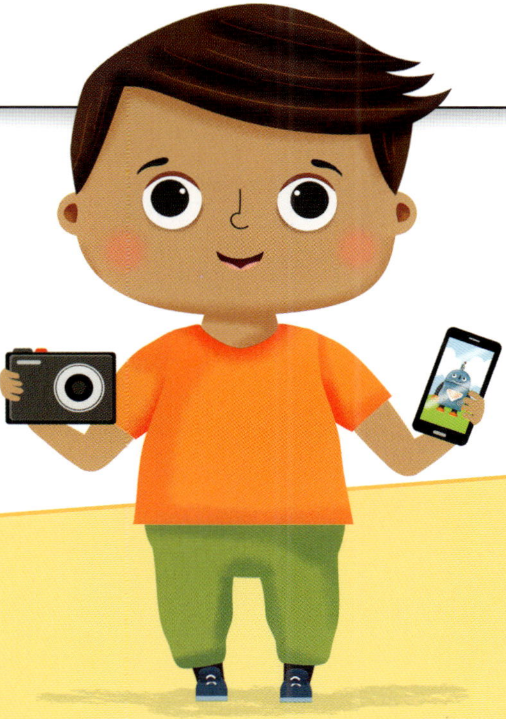

Smartphones look different from digital cameras and do a lot more than just take pictures.

CHAPTER TWO

Taking Great Photos

Now that you know how your camera works, it's time to try taking photos! It takes a lot of time and practice to become a good **photographer**. So don't worry if your pictures don't always look right. It's a good idea to take a lot of pictures. You can delete the ones you don't like later.

Tip 1: Hold steady!

Use two hands when you take pictures. This helps you make sure your camera doesn't shake or move. When you move, your pictures turn out blurry. You can play around with different ways to hold your camera. Try locking your elbows to your side. This can help steady you. Just make sure not to block the lens with your fingers! If your pictures are still too blurry, try propping up your camera on a flat surface. You can use books or a phone stand to help you.

Tip 2: Try a new angle

Try taking pictures from different **angles**. You can shoot from above, looking down. You can lie on the floor and take a photo looking up. You can also try tilting your camera left or right. Try taking a photo of the same object from many different angles, and see how different it looks!

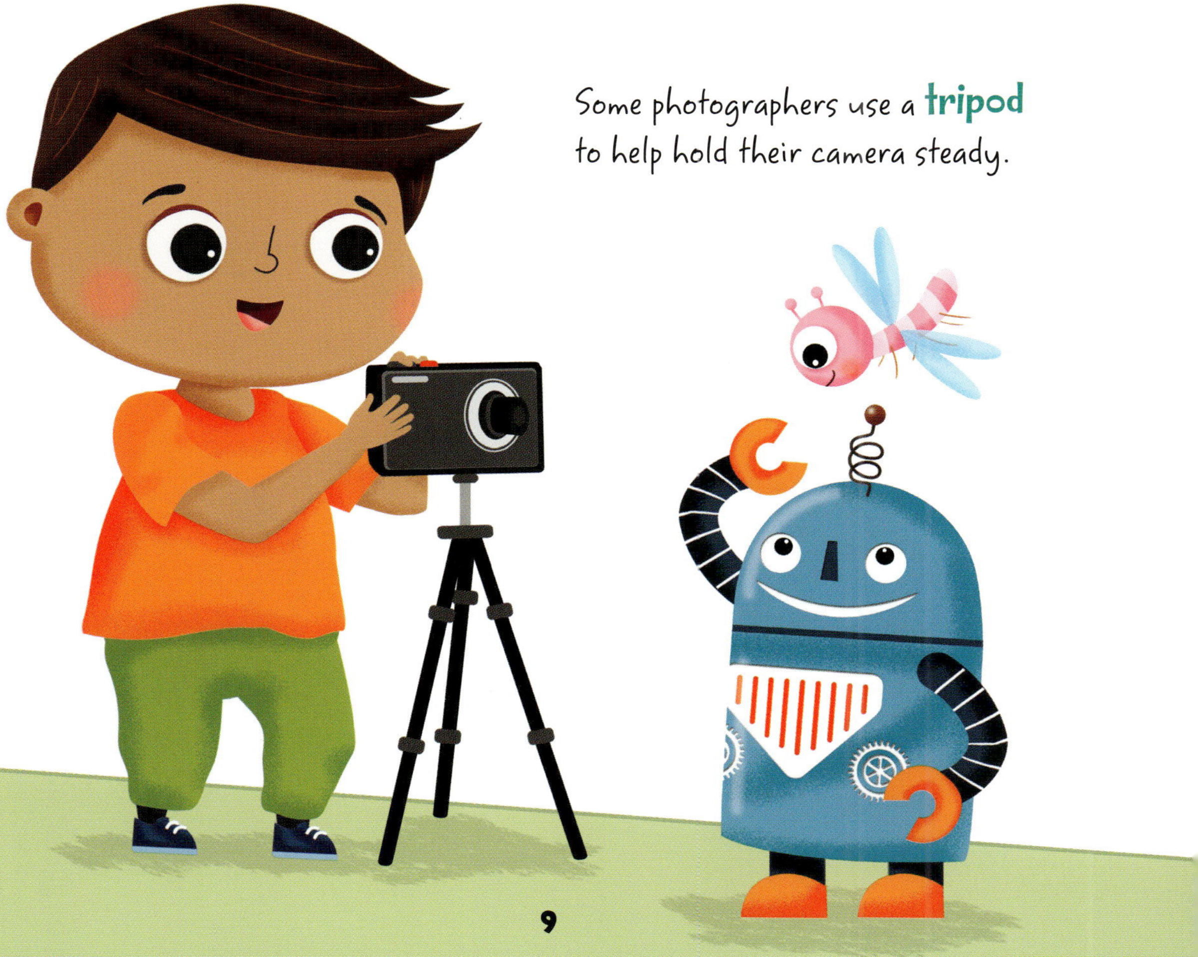

Some photographers use a **tripod** to help hold their camera steady.

Tip 3: Get close or zoom out

Try taking a close-up photo. You can zoom in or move closer to the object. (But it is always best to physically move closer. Your picture will be less clear when you zoom in with your camera.) To get a larger view, try backing up or zooming out. Notice how the picture changes. When you want to see details, a close-up is best. When you zoom out, you can see the bigger picture.

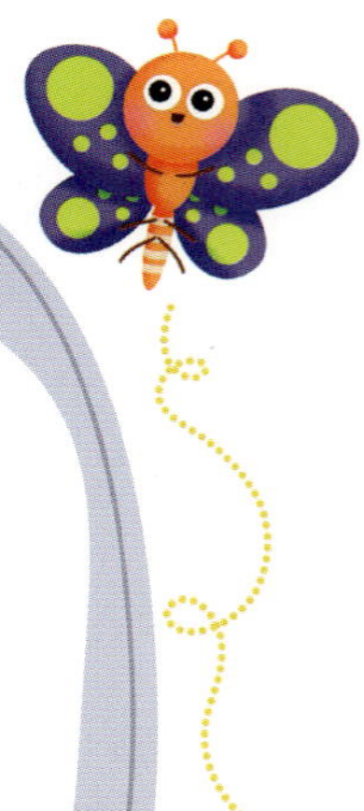

Some **professional** photographers go to school and take classes to become a good photographer. Some get a special degree for photography. Others learn by practicing and taking a lot of pictures. You might want be a professional photographer one day too!

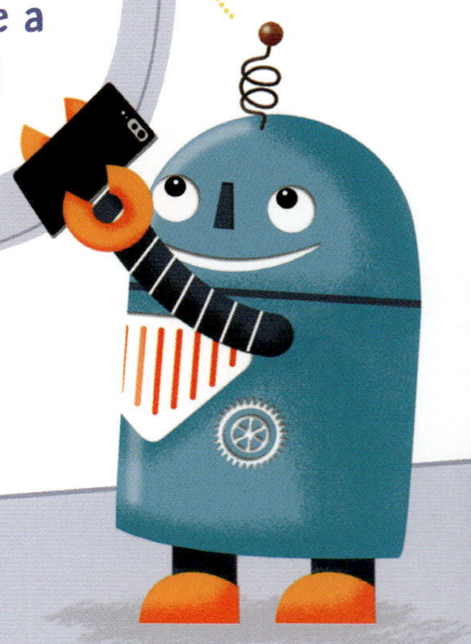

Notice how shooting from different angles can make things look bigger or smaller.

Keep Practicing!

Let's practice these tips for taking good photos. Grab a friend, a pet, or an object to take pictures of. Go outside or find a room with light. Now get ready to take some pictures.

- Take a photo standing above your object.
- Crouch down or lie on the ground, and take a photo from below.
- Take a close-up photo.
- Zoom out and take a photo from far away.
- Prop up your camera and take a picture.
- Try moving your camera while you take a photo.

Which pictures turned out the best? Which ones could be better?

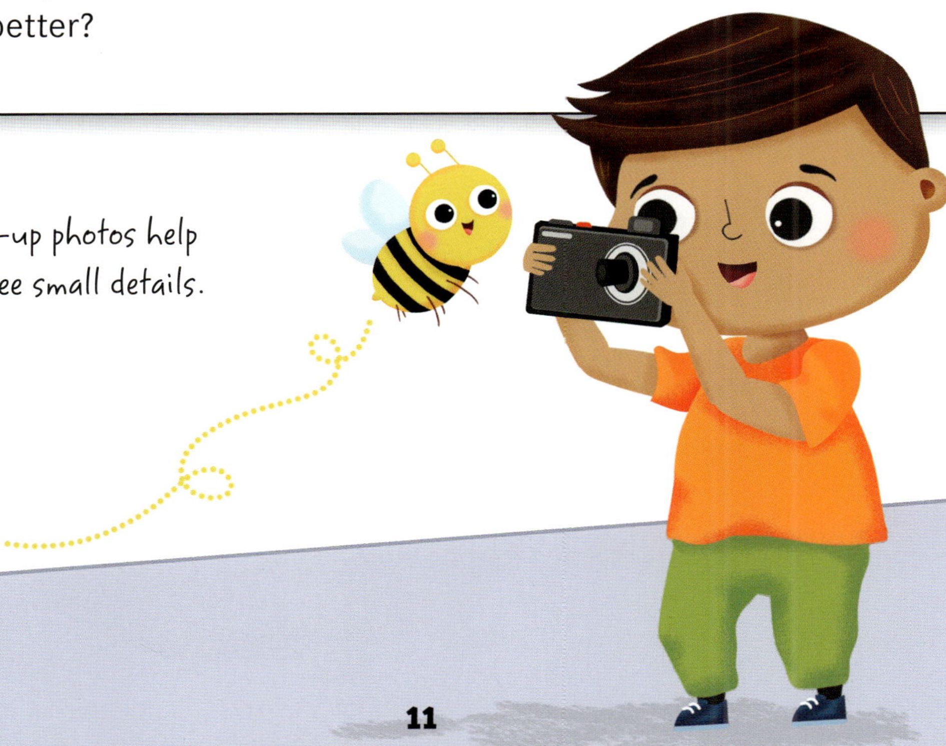

Close-up photos help you see small details.

CHAPTER THREE

Editing Your Photos

Now that you have some photos, it's time to edit them! If you used a smartphone, you can edit them one of two ways. Use either your phone's **gallery** or a photo-editing **app**. If you used a digital camera, an adult can help you **upload** your photos onto the computer. Your computer should have a program to help you edit photos.

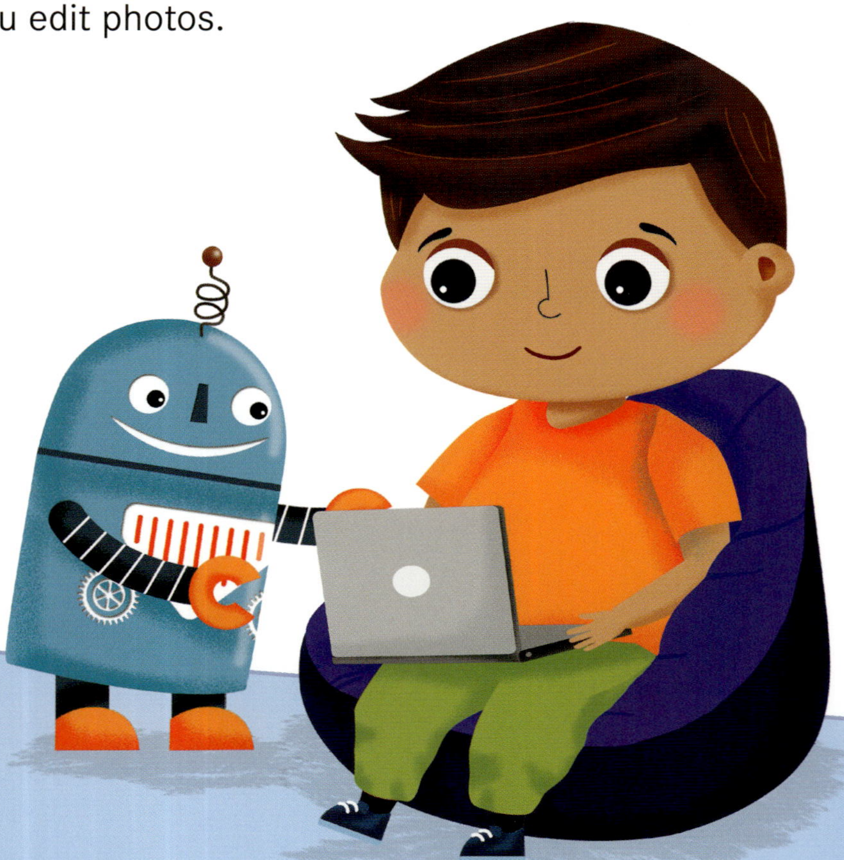

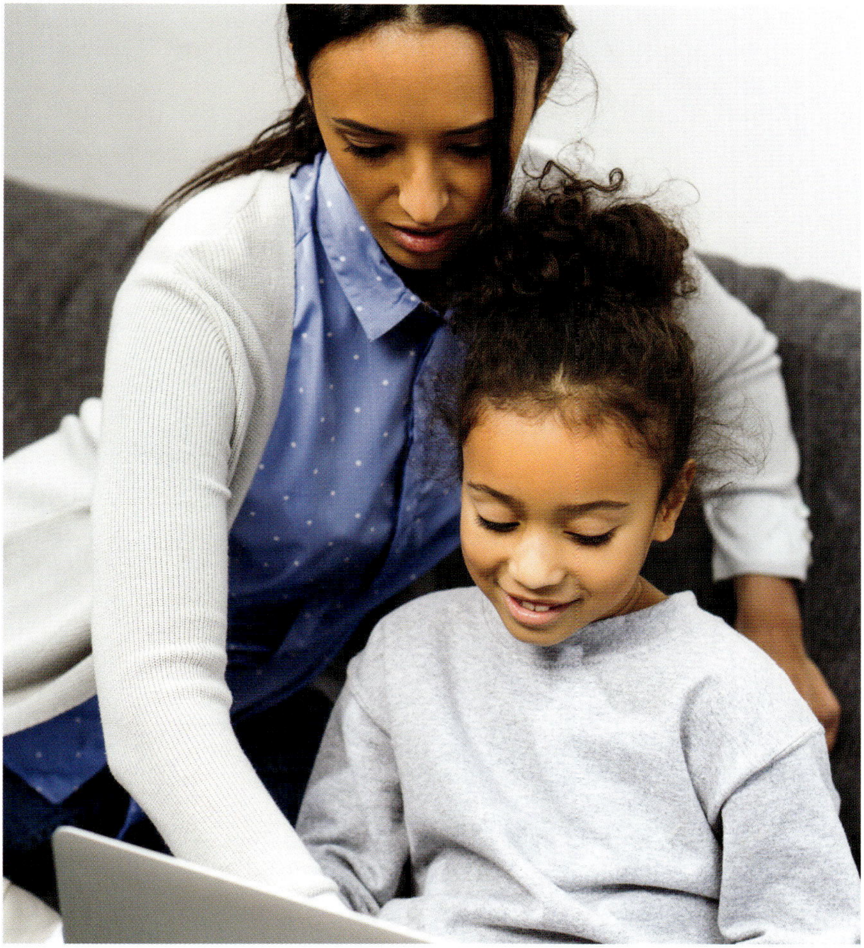

Ask an adult for help downloading a photo-editing app. You can also edit photos in your phone's gallery.

Editing photos can be just as fun as taking them! There are many things you can do with your photos. Here are some things to try:

Cropping:

Cropping your photos helps you take out the parts of the picture that you don't want.

Filters:

If you are using a smartphone, you can add filters to your photos. Filters change the color of your photos. There are so many fun filters to try!

Stickers and text:

You can add text or speech bubbles to your photos. Some apps also let you add stickers or frames to help decorate your photos.

Filters can make your photos look even better.

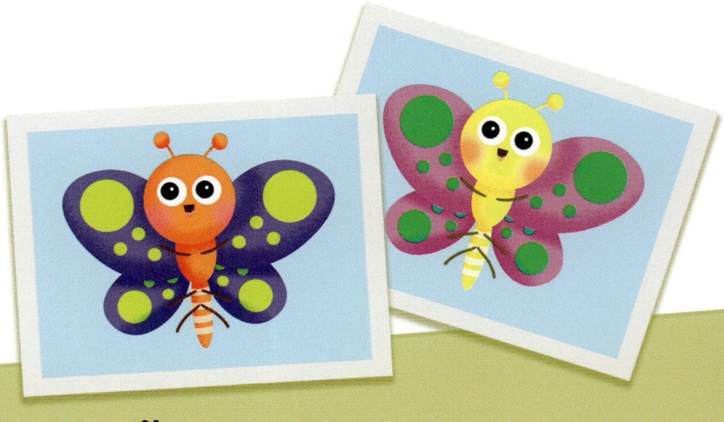

ACTIVITY

It's Time to Edit

If there is something you don't like about your photos, try editing them. Even the best photographers edit their photos! Editing photos fixes things like light and colors. It also adds cool effects.

1. Choose a photo to edit.
2. Have an adult help you open your photo in a photo editor on your computer or smartphone.
3. Crop your photo to the size you want. Take out anything you don't like from the background.
4. Add a filter to your photo.
5. Add some fun stickers and text to your photo.
6. Save your edited photo.
7. Ask an adult to help you share your photo. You can send it through email or post it to your parent's social media. But make sure to ask permission first!

CHAPTER FOUR

Sharing Your Photos

Now that you have edited your photos, you probably want to share them! The easiest and fastest way to do this is online. But don't forget to ask a trusted adult for permission and help first.

You don't have to use social media, like Instagram and Facebook, to share photos. Ask an adult to help you share them with just your trusted friends and family. You can do this using apps like 23snaps and Cluster. Online hosting services like Dropbox and Google Drive can also help you save and share your photos. Only the people you want to see your photos can see them.

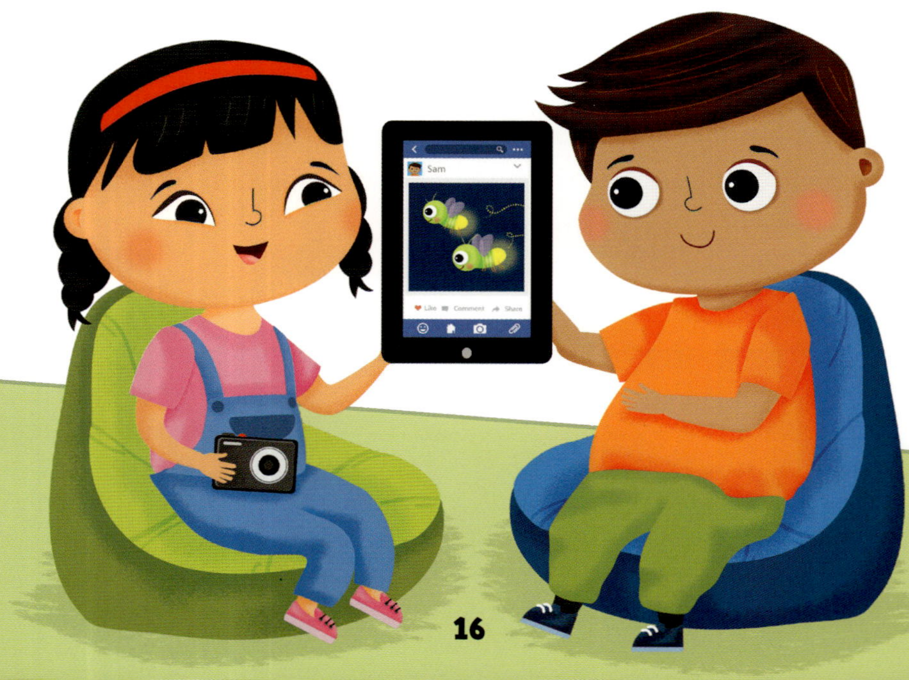

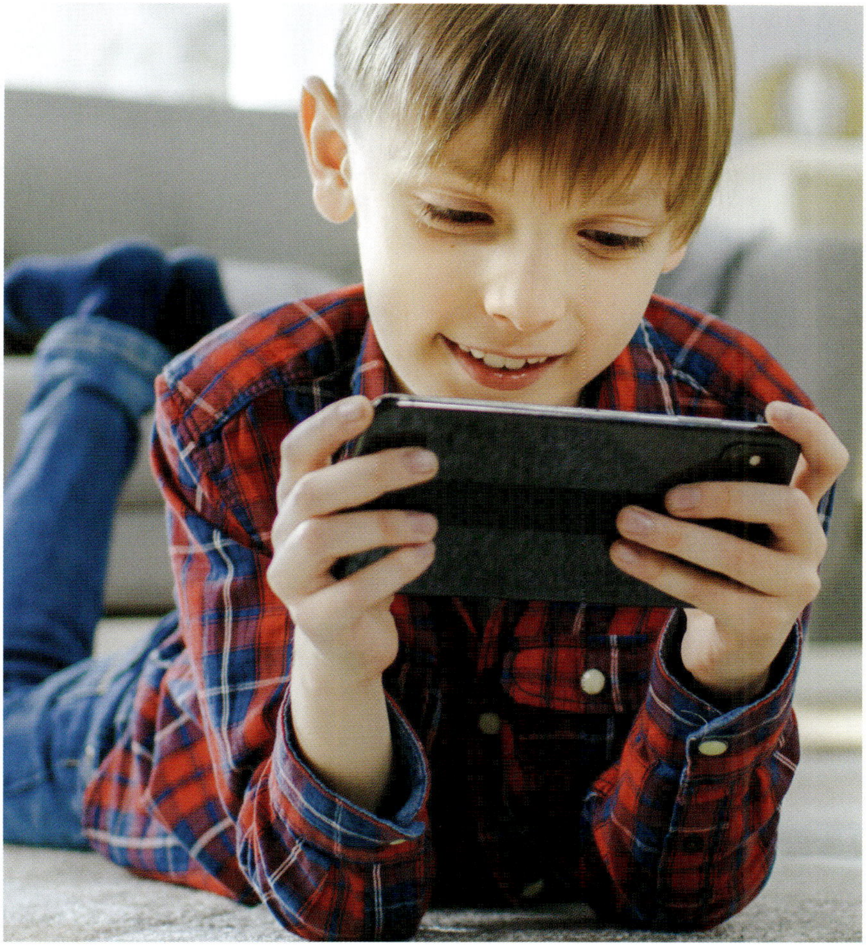

Be careful! Many photo-sharing apps and websites will share your photos with the whole world.

There are other things you can do with your photos too. You can use them to make a **collage** or a scrapbook. You can create a card for a friend. Or print your photos and put them up on your wall to decorate your room.

Many social media sites let you share pictures. The law says you must be at least 13 years old to use these sites. The sites are not meant for kids. So it is better to wait until you are older to use them. Remember, always ask your parents before you post anything online!

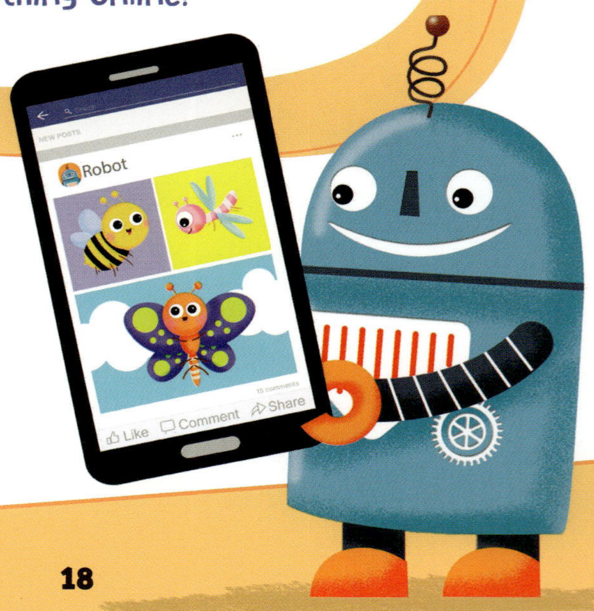

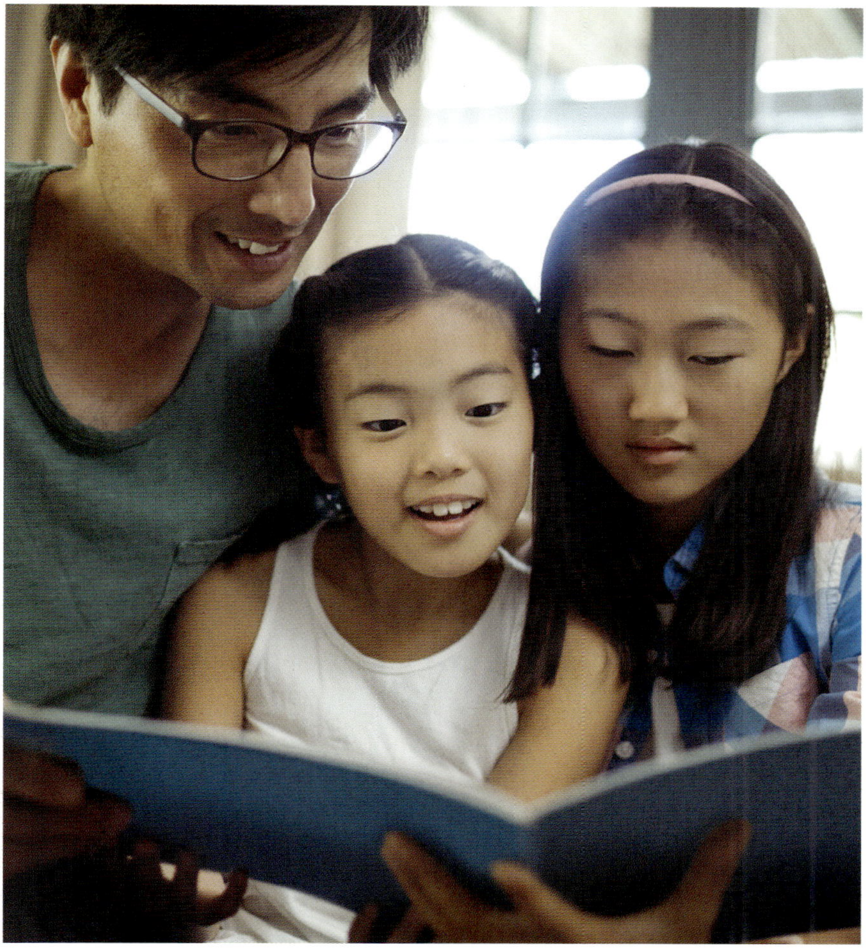

A scrapbook is a great way to save your photos!

ACTIVITY

Make a Slide Show

Let's try making a slide show with your photos! A slide show is a great way to show people your pictures. You can make a slide show on your phone or computer using a program like Google Slides or Microsoft PowerPoint.

1. Add slides to your slide show. You can add as many slides as you want.
2. Add your photos to your slides. You can add multiple photos to each slide, or just one.
3. Add text, decorations, and music to your slides.
4. Play your slide show to see what else you want to add.
5. Once you are happy with your slide show, it's time to share it! Ask an adult to help you email a link to family and friends so they can watch it.

Now you have practiced taking, editing, and sharing pictures. It's a good idea to reflect on what you have learned so far. What else do you want to take pictures of? How can you improve your photos? Keep practicing and you will be proud of the pictures you take!

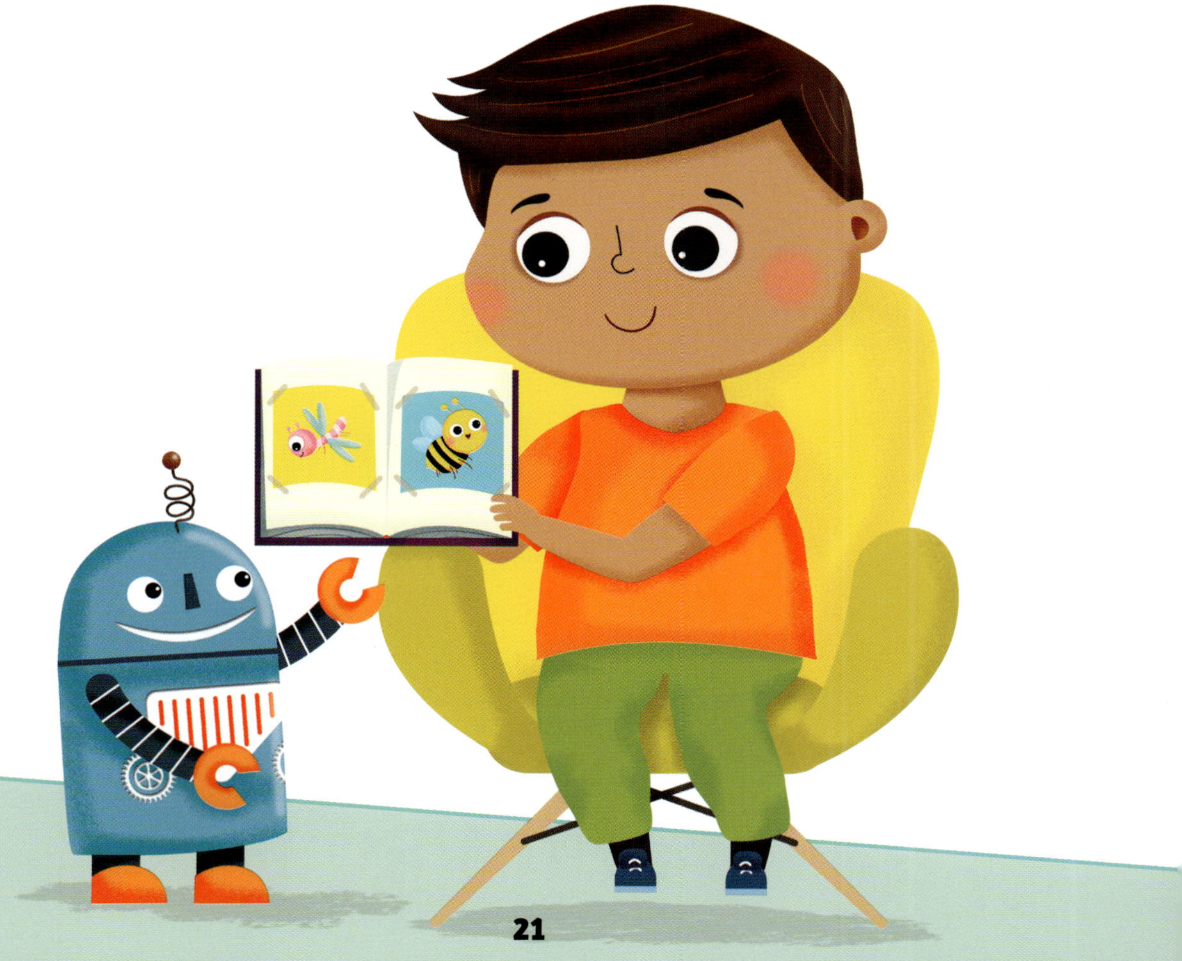

GLOSSARY

angles (ANG-guhlz) positions or points of view

app (APP) a computer program, usually on a smartphone or tablet

collage (kuh-LAHZH) a picture made up of overlapping pictures, words, or other elements

filter (FIL-tur) to remove; also a layer of color or effect you can place on a photo

focuses (FOH-kuhs-iz) changes to make a clear image

gallery (GAL-ur-ee) where your phone stores the pictures you take

lens (LENZ) the eye of a camera

photographer (fuh-TAH-gruh-fur) a person who takes photos for their job

professional (pruh-FESH-uh-nuhl) earning money doing something others do for fun

sensor (SEN-sur) the part of a camera that captures and processes the light from the lens

tripod (TRYE-pahd) a camera stand with three legs

upload (UHP-lohd) to send information from your computer to the internet

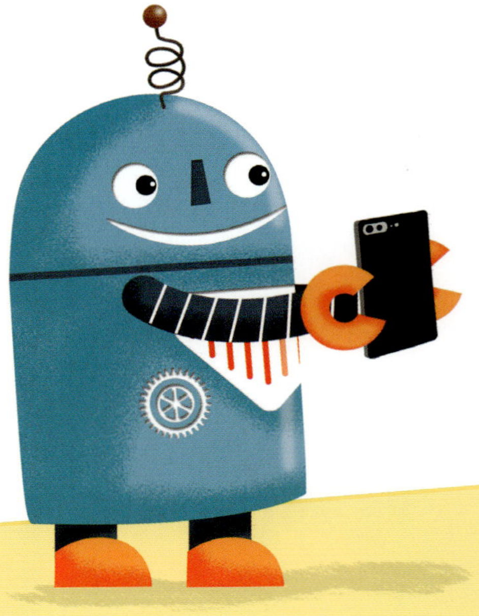

For More
INFORMATION

BOOKS

Honovich, Nancy. *Guide to Photography*. Washington, DC: National Geographic Society, 2015.

Jacquart, Anne-Laure. *Photo Adventures for Kids: Solving the Mysteries of Taking Great Photos*. San Rafael, California: Rocky Nook, 2016.

WEBSITES

Kiddle—Photography Facts for Kids
https://kids.kiddle.co/Photography
Discover more about photography and its history!

Science Kids—Photography
http://www.sciencekids.co.nz/sciencefacts/photography/basicdefinitions.html
Learn more about photography terms.

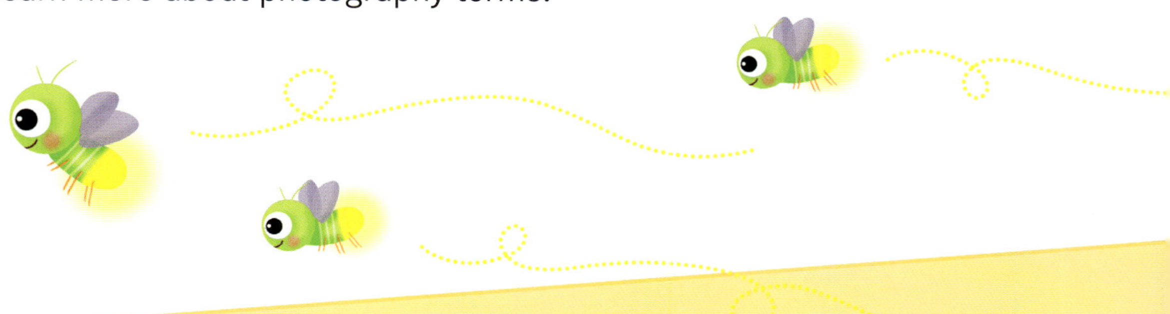

INDEX

About the AUTHOR

Amber Lovett is a certified school librarian and teacher. She lives with her husband, Karan, in Portland, Oregon.